GETTING A RAISE

Made Easy

GETTING A RAISE
Made Easy

Jan Bailey Mattia ■ Patty Marler

Printed on recyclable paper

VGM Career Horizons
a division of *NTC Publishing Group*
Lincolnwood, Illinois USA

Jan

You have challenged me to question my thoughts and ways of
looking at things. After each discussion we have, I look at the
world and myself a little differently.

I thank you for this.

Patty

Library of Congress Cataloging-in-Publication Data

Mattia, Jan Bailey.
    Getting a raise made easy / Jan Bailey Mattia, Patty Marler.
        p.   cm.
    ISBN 0–8442–4345–0 (pbk.)
    1. Promotions.   2. Wages.   3. Negotiation in business.
I. Marler, Patty.   II. Title
HF5549.5.P7M38   1996
650.14—dc20
                                                96–3318
                                                CIP

Published by VGM Career Horizons, a division of NTC Publishing Group
4255 West Touhy Avenue
Lincolnwood (Chicago), Illinois 60646–1975, U.S.A.
© 1996 by NTC Publishing Group. All rights reserved.
No part of this book may be reproduced, stored in a retrieval
system, or transmitted in any form or by any means,
electronic, mechanical, photocopying, recording or otherwise,
without the prior permission of NTC Publishing Group.
Manufactured in the United States of America.

67 8 9 0 VP 9 8 7 6 5 4 3 2 1

Contents

Introduction

Times are tough, employers are cutting expenses—and you want a raise. One of these doesn't seem to fit, but don't give up on your desire for a raise. Your challenge is to make getting a raise fit in with the rest of the factors influencing today's economy. Once you do, you will find yourself at your best, a very productive member of your company's team.

If you make the effort to work through the process of *Getting a Raise Made Easy*, you will be able to make the pieces of the puzzle fit together.

"The first and worst of all frauds
is to cheat oneself."

—Gamaliel Bailey

We begin the process by examining the reasons people avoid requesting raises, the **Shoulda, Coulda, Woulda . . . But** trap. Next we look at **Raise Realities** and take a realistic look at whether or not you should even consider asking for more money.

Who Gets The Raise? takes an objective look at what employers expect from their staff. **Work Hard, Play Hard** looks at how having a well-rounded life increases your chances at obtaining more money. **Increasing Your Price Tag** will help you evaluate how much you are worth to the company. And finally, **Asking For A Raise** describes how to prepare and plan for the big day.

That Was Then . . . This Is Now compares salary requests of today to those of years past.

Once you begin to demonstrate that you deserve more money by increasing your worth at work and proving you are a valuable asset to your company, your employer will have a difficult time turning down your request for a raise.

Begin now. You're on your way to earning more money.

Special Features

Special elements throughout this book will help you pick out key points and apply your new knowledge.

 Notes clarify text with concise explanations.

 Helpful Hints make you stand out in the crowd of raise seekers.

 The **Job Journal** suggests things to keep track of that show how you have contributed to the company.

 The **Process Planner** shows how to improve your performance and worth in the company.

 Special Thoughts provide inspiration and motivation.

You're on your way . . . to earning more money.

Shoulda, Woulda, Coulda…But

Shoulda asked for a raise . . . but

- Why bother? I'll hold out another four years and get a pen set for my ten-year company anniversary.

- I *did* get one of those new company mugs, so I really can't say they never acknowledge my efforts.

Woulda asked for a raise . . . but

- I'm not sure how much money my coworkers are making and I would hate to earn more. It would just be *too* uncomfortable.

- I'm sure if I wait long enough someone will notice how long and how hard I've worked without a salary increase.

- The boss just got back from holidays and I would hate to get her started back to work on the wrong foot.

Coulda asked for a raise . . . but

- My lucky suit is at the dry cleaners and there is just no telling how long it will take them to get that stain off the collar.

- Granted, I just redesigned the company invoicing procedure and saved the organization thousands in lost revenue, but I wouldn't want people to think it had gone to my head.

. . . But?

No buts. Just do it.

Chapter 1

Raise Realities

Back when business was booming and employers were begging for qualified staff, it was not only easy to get jobs, it was easy to secure raises. Today's job market is not so prosperous or companies so loose with the cash. Is it realistic to even think about raises let alone plan for them?

Yes!

Securing a raise is a challenge, but employers who value their employees know it is necessary to keep staff happy—and this often translates into raises. A progressive employer is not surprised when staff request raises. He or she expects it.

"Difficulites show men what they are."

—Epictetus

Even with the large number of qualified people looking for work, *quality* employees are still hard to find. Once they are discovered, employers want to keep them.

Example

AAA Pizza was expanding and advertised for one experienced cook and two food service people. Aware of the local unemployment figures, the managers at AAA thought finding qualified staff would be fast and easy.

Fast, yes. Easy, no. Within one week they received 400 applications, most of these from qualified people. It took several hours to devise a screening method to choose who would be interviewed, and one whole day to read through the applications. Potential applicants were contacted and interviews scheduled.

Interviewing took an additional two days. Finally, three people were chosen to fill the positions. Follow-up meetings were scheduled, salaries were negotiated, and starting dates determined. The light at the end of the tunnel seemed to be growing nearer, but then it faded.

Although each new employee was putting in 110 percent, training them took considerable time and effort. Each person had to become familiar with products, procedures, and customers. Experienced staff took time away from their responsibilities to train new staff and answer questions. Customers received good service, but not the excellent service they were used to.

When the training was finally complete and the new staff could not be picked out from the old, the owners gave a huge sigh of relief. After calculating the cost to advertise, interview, hire, and train new employees, they decided they would do almost anything to keep their current staff . . . even granting raises.

They kept their promise.

 "Desire, ask, believe, receive."
—Stella Terrill Mann

The task of advertising, hiring, and training new employees is a time-consuming and costly process. This is one reason employees get raises, even in a tight job market.

rugal Employers

Although employers know they must give raises to keep valued employees, they don't announce this fact. Companies are in the business of making money, and raises cut into profits.

 Employers know that *not* granting raises eventually cuts into profits even more: unhappy employees, increased sick time, having to train new staff, and so on.

Few employers will go out of their way to offer employees raises. When they do, the raises are usually described as **cost-of-living raises** or increases to keep up with inflation.

2

Cost-of-living and inflation increases, when given, are given to all staff and do not have to be requested individually.

Few employers announce the fact that they may consider giving **performance related increases**. These are raises given for doing a good job. The challenging part is that you must ask for one and, more importantly, convince your employer you deserve one.

 Failing to request a raise may indicate to employers a lack of ambition and initiative. Take the challenge and request a raise when you honestly deserve one.

When approached and convinced, employers will often decide to keep their employees happy and grant an increase, but they still keep their eye on the bottom line. Employers will try to give as little as possible, just enough to keep you, the employee, happy.

Your challenge is to not only convince your employer you deserve a raise, but to convince them to give you as large a raise as possible. If you work hard at it, you may not only get an increase, but a bigger one than you originally expected.

 Keep in mind that your goal is money. If you don't get exactly what you ask for, but still receive an increase, your goal has been reached.

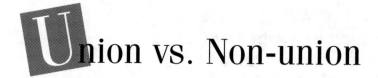

Union vs. Non-union

What about unionized jobs? Aren't the wages set and the increases predetermined?

Yes and no.

Although union jobs have strict salary ranges with predetermined schedules for pay increases, where exactly you fit in these ranges can vary.

Even if you belong to a union where you are given regular pay increases, it is still an excellent idea to chart your progress. Not only will it help you evaluate your strengths and weaknesses, it will give you a concrete record of your accomplishments should you seek other employment.

Example

Jerri has worked for the L.I.L. Rehabilitation Hospital as a unionized social worker for two months. Although the job is what she expected, the salary is not. Jerri decided to do something about it.

Jerri approached R. Bradley, the director of the Social Work Department, and stated that the salary agreed upon when hired was no longer sufficient. Jerri had been doing an excellent job and, although no increase was due according to union guidelines, R. Bradley agreed to see if a raise could be granted.

Several days later R. Bradley returned with the news that when Jerri was hired she had been placed at the bottom of the pay scale for the position. R. Bradley had successfully convinced the Human Resources department that Jerri's past experience and education warranted a move to the top of the pay scale. This was a noticeable pay increase.

Jerri was able to receive a pay increase even in a unionized position.

Although unionized jobs have less flexibility, it is possible to get a raise if your supervisor feels one is warranted. It is still up to *you* to initiate the request.

4

"I never did anything worth doing by accident, nor did any of my inventions come by accident."

—Thomas A. Edison

Non-unionized positions have significantly more salary flexibility. Companies develop their own salary ranges, which are often larger, and moving up requires less red tape. This does not, however, mean it requires less work from you. You still must have initiative and motivation, not only to ask for pay increases, but more importantly, to prove you deserve them.

"I find the great thing in this world is not so much where we stand, as in what direction we are moving."

—Oliver Wendell Holmes

No matter what sort of job you have, it never hurts to request a raise. The key lies in deciding if you deserve one, and then convincing your employer.

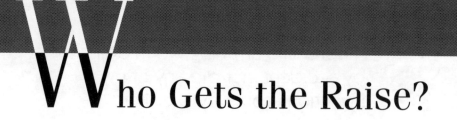

Chapter 2

Who Gets the Raise?

Believe it or not, deciding who will get a raise and who will not is more agonizing for employers than it is for you to ask for one. There is so much to consider.

Ultimately, however, *you* have control over whether or not you will be considered for a raise.

How?

By being a valuable employee! The fact is, employers reward quality staff with pay increases. It is up to you to become the finest employee possible and demonstrate your worth to the company.

Take a good look at what employers want and concentrate on doing your best to become the ideal employee—one who deserves a raise!

Go-Getters

When hiring new staff, employers look for people with initiative and drive, people who will not only get the job done, but who will go above and beyond. Live up to this expectation.

How?

Employers look for someone who:

1. Arrives at work ready to put in a full day and learn as much as possible.

Make it a goal to learn one new thing each day. By making a conscious effort to learn, you will continue to grow and develop as an employee. Log your new knowledge in your job journal.

2. Does the job and does it well. Quality employees take pride in their work, accept only the best from themselves, and never just get by.

3. Is an active participant in discussions and meetings, demonstrating enthusiasm and knowledge.

 Set deadlines even when they have not been assigned by your supervisor. This is a good way to "warm up" to when you will receive assignments with deadlines. It is also a good way to keep your workdays focused. Keep track of whether or not you met your deadlines in your job journal.

4. Offers to lend a hand to co-workers. This shows a willingness to learn more about other positions and improves office morale.

5. Requests increased responsibilities. Employers are impressed by an employee who not only asks for more challenging assignments, but completes them well and on time.

 Be careful not to take on *too* much. While it is good to show your employer that you are ready for bigger and better things, you do not want to be overloaded with work.

6. Takes steps to continue learning and developing new skills.

Employers reward people who do exceptional work. Go-getters get things done. Impress your employer with your drive and enthusiasm, and you improve your odds of getting a raise.

dea Generators

For a company to be competitive and stay alive in the business world, it must continually develop new ideas and products. Naturally, employees who consistently generate ideas are valuable assets.

Think about strategies to improve the way your office is run. Or if you have an idea for a new strategy or product, think it through and develop a proposal. Once your ideas are focused, begin discussing them with your co-workers and supervisors.

 Take care to express your thoughts in a diplomatic way. If at first people are not responsive to your suggestions, do not become discouraged. This is not your cue to keep your mouth shut, but your challenge to encourage others to begin looking at new ways of doing things.

Share your thoughts with your supervisor or boss, and initiate discussions which generate and expand on ideas.

 The employee who stimulates others to think and make suggestions is even more productive than the person who thinks alone.

Although co-workers and even supervisors may seem disinterested or even intimidated when approached with innovative suggestions, it is up to you to be persistent and continue suggesting improvements. Change is the key to any company's prosperity, but few people are comfortable with the initial idea of change.

It may be less initimidating if you voice your suggestions during group discussions. Not only will it be more casual, but group conversations often generate more ideas.

Requests for salary increases by idea generators are taken seriously. Employers need idea people and want them to be part of *their* team, not the competition's.

thical Employees

Simply said, do what is right. Employers value staff who work hard and are dedicated and conscientious in all aspects of their position.

 "The greatest results in life are usually attained by simple means and the exercise of ordinary qualities. These may for the most part be summed up in these two—common sense and perseverance."

—Owen Feltham

Punctuality

If you wonder why you should arrive at work before 8:00 A.M. while others stroll in at 8:15, or why you should take only your scheduled 45 minute lunch even if co-workers are casual about when they return, your answer will come when you approach your boss for a raise.

Many people believe that no one notices a few minutes taken here or there. Although they may not say anything, employers and co-workers *do* make a mental note of your commitment to the workday. Employees who arrive on time and put in a full day are perceived as committed to their jobs.

 Set your alarm 15 minutes earlier in the morning. This will give you a few extra minutes to do some morning stretches and start your day off right.

Employees who are flexible and willing to adjust their lunch break, or those who occasionally arrive early or stay late, are seen in a more favorable light by employers. And they are more likely to receive a raise.

Dependability

Dependability seems as though it should be a straightforward concept, but it's one that takes some effort. Be at work every day, do the work required of you, and meet your deadlines.

 Prioritize your work tasks so that the most important activities are completed first.

When scheduled to work, work.

Sick days are provided by employers as a **benefit**. They are to be used only when you are medically unable to work.

Sick days are not additional holidays to be taken when you don't feel like working. Attending all-night parties and then taking a sick day is not what employers had in mind when they generously granted this benefit.

When at work, work hard.

Give your best and your all. The company will benefit from your work and you can be proud of your accomplishments. Complete your assigned tasks, help your co-workers, and do what you can to make the company better.

 Attend and participate in staff and company meetings. These are opportunities to exchange ideas and learn about what other people are doing.

When given deadlines, meet them.

Deadlines are necessary for a company to be productive and competitive. When you meet your deadlines, the company can meet its own. It's easier for your company to grant a raise when it's making money.

Co-worker Relations

Nothing kills a company's productivity faster than employees fighting amongst themselves. Employers spend a great deal of time hiring people who they believe will be compatible and work well with the other employees. It is important for you to make this a priority as well.

Do what you can to make your work environment a positive and cordial one. Get to know the people you work with and show an interest in the things they do. Take coffee or lunch breaks together and work as part of a team. This not only makes your workplace more productive, it makes it a more interesting place to be.

Keep track of the things you do for co-worker relations, such as buying muffins or organizing a company picnic. Everything you do to make your workplace a fun place to be benefits the company.

Although you have little control over who you work with, you can influence how well you work together. Spend your time working together, rather than resolving conflicts and harboring resentment. Your employer will notice your efforts.

Resolving Conflict

Disagreements will occur on every work site, no matter how well employees get along with each other and with their customers. When a problem arises, it is critical to resolve it quickly.

Describe when and how you have resolved problems with customers. State the outcome and show how your efforts helped the customer and company.

How you resolve a conflict says a great deal about you and your worth to a company. Dealing with disagreement in a calm, cool, and constructive manner demonstrates your willingness to confront problems and your skill in dealing with conflict. People who approach conflict head-on spend less time dwelling on matters and more time on more productive tasks.

Sign up for a Conflict Resolution workshop. Even if your skills in this area are good, you can always learn new techniques and practice old ones.

Employees who work through problems, rather than running to supervisors, are more valuable to a company—and they are more likely rewarded with a raise.

Office Politics

Companies are run according to the way the management thinks works best. Unfortunately, this is not always consistent with what *you* feel works best. While it is a good idea to voice your ideas and suggestions, it does not help you to dwell on matters you cannot change. People who constantly criticize the way things are done bring down office morale and hinder productivity.

When you go for a coffee break and the discussion turns to cutting down a procedure, project, or employee, initiate a discussion on how to deal with the problem instead of joining in the criticism. You will be remembered as the person who came up with the solution, and it is the problem-solver who is valued by employers.

Make suggestions for improvement. If they are followed up on, great. If not, *move on*.

Confidentiality

Respecting the confidentiality of clients, customers, co-workers, and the company is an important and often overlooked component of a positive work ethic.

Example

When Chris Wilson was prescribed a medication, she did not want anyone at work to know about it. Because it would not affect her performance at work, she felt it was really no one's concern.

While Chris was taking her medicine with a glass of water from the cooler at work, a co-worker came up and asked her if she was feeling all right. When Chris quietly answered that she was fine, her co-worker announced in a loud voice how he hated to have to take prescribed drugs for anything, because one never knew what the side effects would be.

The next thing Chris knew there were two more people at the cooler, curious about the discussion and wanting to share their views.

 No matter how interesting it may sound, you must respect confidential information, whether it is personal or directly related to the job.

It is often difficult to determine with whom you should discuss certain aspects of your job. You want to be sure you don't intrude on people's rights by discussing things they do not want discussed.

 If you are unsure about whether or not to discuss a subject, follow this rule: **"When in doubt, keep your mouth closed."**

There may also be projects at work that need to be kept under wraps. You don't want to be responsible for your company losing a big project because you discussed it with a friend who told a competitor who, as a result, underbid your company. Not only will you *not* get a raise, you may not even have a job afterwards.

"The integrity of men is to be measured by their conduct, not by their professions."

—Junius

Respect your company's and other people's right to privacy.

Being an ethical employee is key to being a responsible, reliable, and dependable employee. It is also a fundamental consideration for employers when deciding whether or not you deserve a raise.

Specialists vs. Generalists

You might wonder if employers want their staff to be specialists in their position only or generalists who know something about each aspect of the company. As staff numbers shrink, and more demands are placed on the remaining employees, the trend is toward employees becoming generalists in the workplace, with specific areas of expertise. In other words, a combination of specialist and generalist.

The First Step

When you begin a new position, it will take time to become familiar with what is expected of you and to become proficient at your job. During this initial learning period, become a specialist by concentrating on your position.

When you have spare time, discover more about your job and its place and function within the company. Read relevant literature or try something new on your computer. Explore avenues that will help you do a better job in the long run.

The initial learning period may be anywhere from a few weeks to a few years. Ask experienced staff how long it took them to become skilled at their job.

The Next Step

After you have a good understanding of your position and what it involves, and are able to do your tasks well, it is time to become a generalist. Discover what others in your department and your office do and occasionally try your hand at their job. Help out co-workers, take on extra responsibilities, or "trade" jobs for a few hours. The experience will be an invaluable learning tool, and it will be stimulating as well.

Obtain the approval of your employer before you trade duties with a co-worker. Explain that you have a good understanding of your job and would like to learn more about other positions.

When you ask for a raise, you might be in the process of specializing or generalizing. If you are specializing, emphasize that you are focusing your efforts and want to concentrate on doing your job well before learning more about what others do.

You do not have to be an expert in your field before you request a raise. Learning a new position takes more effort than performing tasks once you are competent. Developing your skills is as good a reason for a raise as being an expert.

If you are generalizing, state that you have a good grasp of your responsibilities and position. Describe how you have begun expanding your knowledge of the company and what others do.

Either way, your employer will be impressed with your efforts and the reasoning behind what you are doing.

 Remember, your job duties must not suffer while you are working to generalize your skills.

ompany Promoters

Employees who speak positively about their company and promote the business are valuable advertising tools. Promotions are expensive. The more word-of-mouth advertising *you* do, the less your company has to pay advertising agencies.

When requesting a raise, describe how you are saving the company money through your efforts. At the very least, you are increasing awareness of the company. Explain that you promote products and services, and describe how you represent the organization in a positive way.

 Wear company hats or pins and always speak favorably about your company. Recommend your company's products and services to friends. Work hard to generate new business.

If at all possible, give concrete examples of business the company has gained through your personal efforts. Any advertising you do is potential savings for the company, so don't underestimate what you can contribute.

Knowledgeable Employees

Employees who know what their company does are very important to businesses. It is virtually impossible for you to have an impact when you are uncertain of how your position "fits" within the organization. Be sure you have a clear understanding of what the organization you work for does, how the company does it, who the customers or clients are, and how your position is important to accomplishing company goals.

Familiarize yourself with your company's mission statements, mandate, policies, and procedures. Know the "ins" and "outs" of the business, so you can represent it in the best way possible.

Make it part of your job to be informed and accurate about your organization. This in itself will make you a valuable employee.

Competition-Smart Employees

Do you know who your competitors are and what they are doing? It is hard to say your product is better than theirs if you don't know what they are selling or for how much. Stay on top of your competitors.

How?

1. Compare your company to others and figure out why you are doing better or worse than they are. This is called **bench marking**. If you discover a way to improve your company's sales or image, this is the time to be an idea generator and bring your suggestions and insights to your supervisor's attention.

2. Know the names and products of the other companies. Then when customers compare products, you will be able to provide constructive evaluations on how your product compares to others.

Avoid speaking negatively about another company's services and products. It is unprofessional. Instead, discuss how great your own products are. Customers will feel that you have a superior product, and not think that you have to undermine the competition to secure sales.

3. Get to know employees who work for the competition. You will discover more about their products and services, which will help you make comparisons. It may also come in handy should you ever be looking for another job.

Staying on top of your industry is beneficial to you and your employer, so take the time to bench mark.

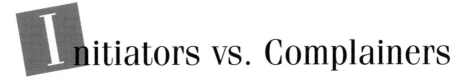

Initiators vs. Complainers

Initiators recognize problems, look for ways to resolve them, and implement change. That is why they are highly valued by the companies they work for. Complainers, on the other hand, waste valuable time and energy grumbling and have little to show for their efforts.

When you find yourself in the middle of a venting session at work, make the effort to say "Now what are we going to do about this?" Be the person who initiates the discussion on how to take positive steps toward changing things.

Employers respect employees who develop solutions to problems. When you suggest a change, provide strategies for making the change possible. Avoid simply demanding things without giving concrete ideas on how to make them possible.

An employee who offers constructive and clear strategies leaves his or her employer free to concentrate on more important tasks—like taking your raise request seriously!

Ongoing Learners

What you have learned so far—in school or on the job—has brought you to where you are today. Continuing to grow will get you to where you want to be tomorrow.

"Thinking is the hardest work there is, which is the probable reason why so few engage in it."

—Henry Ford

Business is continually changing. The valuable employee makes it her responsibility to stay on top of those changes.

How?

1. Read relevant literature and stay current with new concepts and procedures. Discover what is happening with competitors and search for ways to improve your company.

2. Attend conferences, seminars, or professional development meetings. Learn new techniques and concepts, and continue to grow as an employee.

 "Folks who never do any more than they get paid for, never get paid for any more than they do."

—Elbert Hubbard

3. Sign up for workshops. Personal development and work-related courses allow you to continue growing and are an excellent way to motivate yourself to try new things.

4. Attend in-services and staff meetings. Pay attention to what is happening within your company.

5. Access the computer network to discover the newest and latest information in your field. This is a fast and fun way to obtain current facts about your industry.

Do what you can to continue learning. It will not only make you a better employee, it will make you a more knowledgeable person in general.

 **Money Savers**

One thing *every* business has in common is accounting. Companies that manage their books well stay in business, while those which do not quickly disappear. Managers and business people are constantly looking for ways to make money. Saving money is one way to do this.

Cost-reduction techniques can be anything from cutting back on the quality of paper used during photocopying to changing the courier who delivers your product.

Any steps you take to save your company money will be noticed. Search out and implement money-saving techniques and make suggestions on how to streamline operations. Cost-cutting techniques can often be implemented with little impact on day-to-day operations.

Keep track of the supplies you purchase and the procedures which cost the company money. Seek out less expensive alternatives, calculate how much money the company could save, and inform your supervisor of your discoveries. Your interest and initiative will be appreciated.

Nothing impresses employers more than ideas on how to save the company money. The money saved today may go towards your raise tomorrow.

Document any money-saving ideas you have suggested or implemented.

Summing Things Up

Employers place high expectations upon their employees and seek out and reward the best people. In doing the best you can, you become an asset to your employer—and someone they want to keep. An employer who believes you are an exceptional employee is more easily convinced that you deserve a raise.

"We cannot escape fear. We can only transform it into a companion that accompanies us on all our exciting adventures. Take a risk a day—one small or bold stroke that will make you feel great once you have done it."

—Susan Jeffers

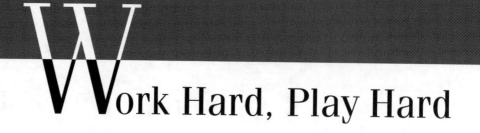 Work Hard, Play Hard

Why is there a chapter about recreation and "playing" in a book on getting a raise?

The answer is simple.

**People who play and do things they enjoy are more productive.
Productive people are valued by employers.
Employers give raises to people they value!**

A simple enough concept, but one which is often ignored.

 "You will do foolish things, but do them with enthusiasm."

—Colette

Play To Be More Productive?

Somehow we have been brainwashed into believing that productive people are those who spend their lives eating, drinking, and sleeping work. Are the workers who leave the office two hours after quitting time, their briefcases filled with work to complete at home, somehow better than us? And are they truly more productive?

The work put out in a measly eight-hour day could not *possibly* come close to what they accomplish daily, weekly, or yearly? Or could it?

Example

Picture the person who leaves work with briefcase in hand. His or her day may look something like this:

7:00 A.M.	Leave for work.
7:15 A.M.	Dictate a letter while driving to work.
7:45 A.M.	Arrive at work before everyone else for quiet working time.
8:30 A.M.	Begin the normal work day.
12:00 P.M.	Have lunch with a client.
1:30 P.M.	Return to work.
5:00 P.M.	Take one hour to work quietly and get those "must finish" jobs done. Pack briefcase.
6:00 P.M.	Drive home.
6:45 P.M.	Have dinner.
8:00 P.M.	Complete the finer details which never seem to get done at work.
11:30 P.M.	Go to bed exhausted.

When do they recuperate and spend time doing things for themselves?

"We have too many people who live without working and we have altogether too many who work without living."

—Charles R. Brown

Work alone is not enough to keep people going. It is a necessary and fundamental part of our lives, but it is not the *only* part. People must experience a variety of things in life to remain stimulated, interested, and productive.

Consider

Habituation is a process in which people are exposed to an experience so often that they become bored and no longer notice or react to it.

Example

Think of how you felt the day you received your first paycheck. You may have studied it carefully, thrilled to see your work turn into hard-earned cash. Or maybe you rushed to the bank because you knew exactly how you were going to spend every cent.

Now think about yesterday when you frantically ran to the bank to deposit your check before the mortgage payment was withdrawn. Your $1000 paycheck today is nowhere near as exciting as your first $125 check was.

This is habituation. And **dishabituation** is the process by which we begin to react to the experience again.

Example

Think about when you were unemployed for several months and then secured work again. Your first paycheck from the new employer was a lot more exciting than previous checks, but still not as exciting as the first one from your first job was.

These concepts give us a glimpse into why it is so important to play as well as work.

 "It's good to have money and the things that money can buy, but it's good, too, to check up once in a while and make sure that you haven't lost the things that money can't buy."

—George Horace Lorimer

Habituation at Work

People who work continuously and take no time to relax, enjoy themselves and rejuvenate become habituated with work. At first they may show signs of increased productivity, but these signs quickly disappear.

The overworked person appears to be running and doing so much, but in reality he or she is easily distracted, taking frequent breaks for daydreaming. Less actual work is accomplished. What an average employee completes in several hours may take an overworked employee all day. The **quantity** of work suffers.

There will occasionally be days or weeks when you must put in additional time to complete a project, meet a deadline, or learn a new job. The key is to not make a habit of it.

The **quality** of work suffers as well. The finished job no longer reflects the enthusiasm and creativity of past projects. The job is tiring and repetitive to the overworked employee, and it shows in their lack of enthusiasm.

A Critical Look at Overworkers

Overworking is counterproductive, with less work being completed and the quality suffering. It's hard to believe that people who work so hard are actually doing less than the average employee. How could this be?

"Leisure for men of business, and business for men of leisure, would cure many complaints."

—Esther L.S. Thrale

What you see

Stacks of telephone messages, which are taken to be a sign of importance and the demands on the overworkers' time.

The "tons" of work still to do.

What's really happening

They can't find the energy to return calls, so messages keep piling up. Over half the messages are from people who have called more than once.

The overworker is easily distracted and can't finish a single thing until everyone goes home. The work completed is actually equal to what you do.

The overworkers' secretaries work a great deal harder than yours.	The overworkers need pseudo-baby-sitters to constantly remind them of deadlines and appointments. Their secretaries must organize the overworkers' time, as well as their own. The typing being completed is for a project that was received today but due yesterday.
Someone who appears to be very important to the company.	The company used to think so, but now the workaholic seems to be running in circles. The company gives an "A" for effort, but a "C+" for the quality of work.

 Become more organized. Write "to do" lists and complete *all* the tasks on your list.

What you don't see

- The time wasted daydreaming (the overworkers might call it "thinking"), because they can't concentrate for more than a few minutes.
- The full wastepaper basket, because the memos they are trying to write aren't coming out right.
- The tenth cup of coffee consumed in the past two hours.
- The angry clients because the overworker doesn't return calls.
- The medical and prescription bills from stress-related illnesses.
- The scotch flask tucked away in the briefcase to help relax after a stressful day.
- The lack of genuine interest in work.

 "The man who has lived longest is not the man who has counted most years, but he who has enjoyed life most."

—Jean Jacques Rousseau

Not only does the overworked person have no time to themselves, they have no time for family and friends. They no longer know who they are (other than being an employee for XYZ company). They lose touch with their family and have no friends to turn to.

 "Karoshi" is the Japanese word for the phenomenon of "death by overworking."

It is counterproductive to overwork. What's more, it does little for your chances of getting a raise. Instead of putting in low quality extra hours, go home and play, and tomorrow be productive for eight hours.

So You Already Work Too Much

If the description of an overworker sounds like you, don't despair. You *can* change the direction of your life. Begin by making time to do things for yourself and to enjoy living again. Make small changes, and eventually it will get easier. It may be necessary to have someone help you make these crucial changes, but be persistent.

 "Work as though you would live forever, but live as though you would die today."

—St. Edmund of Canterbury

You will begin to notice a difference in the quality and quantity of your work, and so will your employer. The flair will return and you will be a happier and more productive employee. And remember, it is the **productive** employee who receives the raise.

What Is Playing Hard?

Playing hard means doing things you enjoy: things that make you feel good, that excite you, that you crave. When an activity fills these needs, you are playing hard.

The key lies in discovering what these things are.

"True enjoyment comes from activity of the mind and exercise of the body; the two are ever united."

—Alexander Humboldt

If you already know of activities—not chores—you would like to do, then do them. If you have an interest in something new, try it. There is no better time than the present to act on those "someday I'd like to try . . ." thoughts.

Make it your personal goal to never have to say "I wish I would have tried . . ." Try it *now*!

If you don't know where to start, begin by looking for things that interest you.

How?

✔ Remember the things that you used to enjoy. Do you think these activities are still interesting? Give them a try again and see if they are as much fun as they once were.

✔ Plan to do something physical. Although this may be the last thing you want to do when you feel tired, physical activity is stimulating. You will be surprised by the extra energy you have when done.

It's amazing how one can be physically exhausted, go to bed, and wake up the next day feeling mentally sharp.

✔ Visit a store that carries magazines. Many magazines concentrate on crafts, sports, and other activities, and you may discover an interest you never knew you had.

Look at magazine covers and see if something catches your eye. Buy the magazine and browse through it. If you are still interested, try the activity.

✔ Tag along with a friend. If your friend enjoys flying remote-control gliders, maybe you will too. If not, at least you've spent enjoyable time socializing.

Do not consider watching television to be leisure. TV numbs the brain and provides little mental stimulation. Try disconnecting your cable to free up time for more constructive activities. It will also give you some extra money for new interests.

✔ Review your local community calendar. Sign up for activities or workshops—just for the fun of it!

Keep an open mind when you try new things. You may even discover some new things about yourself.

When?

Schedule time for non-work-related activities and stick to it. Allow yourself at least a couple of hours per week. Even better, schedule time each day.

"Always leave enough time in your life to do something that makes you happy, satisfied, even joyous. That has more of an effect on economic well-being than any other single factor."

—Paul Hawken

Take your leisure seriously and commit to following through on your "fun" plans. It may take effort to organize your work, chores, and family to allow time to play, but the effort will be worth it. It is as important to play as it is to pay the bills—for you and for your productivity at work.

Summing Things Up

Leave your work at the workplace, take time for yourself, and never underestimate the value of leisure time. Be sure to include fun activities in your life. The benefits will be apparent in your health, your personal life, and your work.

"We live in deeds, not years; in thoughts, not breaths; in feelings, not in figures on the dial; we should count time by heart-throbs. He most lives who thinks most, feels the noblest, acts the best."

—Gamaliel Bailey

Fun is necessary, so take it seriously!

Chapter 4

Increasing Your Price Tag

The economy is tough, companies are cutting back and streamlining their organizations, the cost of living is increasing, and you need more money to cope. You aren't the only one in the company feeling the crunch of inflation, however. So why do *you* deserve a raise?

"There is the risk you cannot afford to take, [and] there is the risk you cannot afford not to take."

—Peter Drucker

Business is changing, and therefore our attitude towards business and how we fit into the business world must change as well. We are not *entitled* to a high-paying job simply because we live in an industrialized nation with a relatively high standard of living.

More than ever, industry operates on an exchange basis: skills and or knowledge are traded for money, period. If you have the most knowledge and expertise in your particular field, you make the most money. If your skills are current, your knowledge is cutting edge, and your attitude is progressive, you will be a valuable asset for any organization.

If you are wondering if you deserve more money, there is only one real issue: What do you have to offer in exchange?

"Undoubtedly, we will become what we envisage."

—Claude M. Bristol

Determining Your Price Tag

Evaluating yourself is always a difficult thing. Evaluating yourself and attaching a dollar figure to it is even more challenging. Nevertheless, this is exactly what you must do when considering asking for a salary increase.

Progress Checks

Your role at work should be one of constant learning and growth. As with any learning process, there must be some way to check your progress along the way. If there are no evaluations, exams, or reviews, it is impossible to know if you are doing, learning, providing, or surpassing what is expected.

Does your employer provide these checks?

What?

Regular performance reviews

Possibly the single most important feedback tool, a performance review is a chance to sit down one on one with your employer and discuss your job performance in its entirety. This **information exchange** should be documented (and both you and your employer given a copy), so time-lines, agendas, goals for improvement, and constructive criticism can be followed up on at subsequent reviews.

Performance reviews are also used to document **positive performance**. Take note of all the positive things your employer has to say about you and build on them. If your workplace does not incorporate regular reviews, take it upon yourself to meet with your employer or supervisor to evaluate your performance every three or six months.

 If no other avenues are available, you should incorporate and request all progress checks during your performance review.

Individual goal setting sessions

If you or your employer do not set concrete and achievable goals, it is difficult to chart and evaluate progress of *any* kind. During your performance review, or at any other set meeting time, sit down with your employer or supervisor and discuss company objectives, how they relate to you, and how your position relates to those objectives.

These goals should be:

- Written down

- Achievable within a restricted time

- Measurable

- Progressive

They should also take into consideration concrete duties, as well as the more intangible "people skills" needed to be an effective team player.

 Take time to set and reset your personal goals, in addition to those you set with your employer. Use these clearly stated goals as continual progress checks, and note when they are accomplished in your job journal.

Team or department goal setting

It is very difficult to steer a ship when the crew is pointing the sails in several different directions. In order to achieve your goals, the entire team must be working toward the same objective. Make the effort to sit down regularly with the rest of the department to check your progress as a group, re-chart the course if necessary, and discuss your contribution as a member of the team.

Product knowledge and awareness of company policy

Do you know your product and your company? There is no way around this essential question. If you lack basic knowledge about the company you work for and its customers, products, or services, perhaps you should reevaluate your argument for deserving a raise.

Are you aware of recent changes in company production, policy, or objectives? Make a point of scanning the bulletin board and reading company literature.

Direct consumer feedback

Consumer feedback is excellent, but obviously only available in certain industries. If you are in an industry where you deal with the public, know that your employer will take a customer's opinion of your performance seriously. Always look for ways to improve your customer service skills, and make a considered effort to implement the suggestions and feedback you receive from clients and customers.

Be sure to add positive customer comments or correspondence to your job journal. These are evidence of how valuable an employee you are.

Peer group evaluations

Employers are faced with the challenging task of building teams of people who not only have the concrete skills to work together, but also have the ability to relate well to each other on a personal level. Although your co-workers are not responsible for granting you a raise, it is important that they regard you as a positive and productive member of the team and convey that feeling to your employer.

Most likely your employer will provide you with feedback and suggestions on how to improve your value at work. This should be an information exchange, and *you* must spend time thinking about how you could increase your worth and present these suggestions at your meeting.

Your employer will be impressed with your commitment to improvement and your honest attempt at evaluating your own performance.

"Shoot for the moon. Even if you miss it you will land among the stars."

—Les Brown

If your workplace does not provide for these various progress checks, take it upon yourself to ask your employer for regular feedback. The meeting when you ask for a raise is certainly a good time to ask for constructive criticism regarding your performance, but receiving this information on a regular basis is essential to improving your worth at work.

Self-Evaluation

When you ask for a raise you will be expected to justify to your employer, with concrete examples, what you have done for the organization, where you rate, and what makes you "worth" more than you currently receive.

Unless you belong to a union, it is no longer enough to ask for, or expect, more money simply because you have been with the company for a certain period of time.

Sit down with a pencil and paper and ask yourself some realistic questions about your work. Consider your:

■ On-the-job performance

■ Work ethic

■ Workstyle

■ Work habits

■ Productivity

■ Effectiveness as part of the team

■ Bottom line dollar contribution to the organization

Be sure to write in pencil. This is a growth process and we don't want anything written down that can't be changed!

Remember that your attitude and contribution to positive team interaction are worthwhile contributions to an organization, as well as the concrete work you do.

Begin by answering some general questions about your job performance.

What?

1. Do my co-workers like and respect me and my opinion in the workplace? What do I do to influence this?

2. Am I a positive and professional part of the organization? How?

Make an honest effort to be objective about yourself and your performance. Try to evaluate yourself from the perspective of your employer.

3. When there are problems at work, do I accept responsibility when appropriate? Do I offer solutions when possible?

Think of examples to support your answers and write them in your job journal. Concrete examples make what you say much more believable.

4. Do I move toward increased responsibility on the job or do I simply do only what is required of me?

5. Am I aware of the workings of the rest of the company? Do I know where my company stands within the industry?

6. Do I make a conscious effort to improve my work performance, increase my knowledge level, and maintain a competitive edge? How?

7. Am I the type of person who honestly looks for ways to improve company efficiency? Or do I simply wait to be told of new ways to do things?

8. Do I work to expand my job description, increase my responsibilities, and become a more valuable employee? How?

There is a delicate balance between evaluating yourself in the workplace and unfairly comparing yourself to others. Although you must consider your role as a member of a team, do not fall into the trap of continually comparing yourself to others.

Do not constantly criticize your performance and think of all the things you have done wrong, not completed, done too slowly, or had to do over in your term of employment.

Do pay attention to all the positive things you have contributed to the job, from concrete, easily measured things, to your attitude and personal impact in the workplace. Remember that not everything is always under your control. Make a habit of looking for the good things in your performance before you look for the things that need to be worked on. You will be surprised at how this small habit will change your outlook.

So you organized the company slow pitch tournament and entered the office gang in a charity bowling game. Don't underestimate the value of these things in the eyes of your employer. Arranging outside activities takes work and a genuine interest, and your employer knows it.

As individuals we all have different strengths and weaknesses. Work hard to acknowledge both in yourself.

Working toward and asking for a raise is about *your* contribution to the company and requires self-awareness. You will need to ask yourself a series of questions.

Am I:

- Punctual?
- Productive?
- Aware?

- Responsible?
- Reliable?
- Loyal?
- Interested?
- Innovative?
- Focused?
- Positive?
- Professional?
- Competitive?
- Cooperative?
- Proactive?
- Cost-conscious?

 Avoid answering these questions with a mere "yes" or "no." Practice more elaborate responses that would help you convince others that what you say is true.

Do I:

- Offer solutions when there are problems?
- Take initiative?
- Take pride in my work?
- Accept challenges and additional responsibility when presented?
- Enjoy the work I do?
- Regularly set personal and professional goals and work to achieve them?
- Accept criticism and feedback and make appropriate changes?
- See value in what I am doing?
- Keep the objectives and needs of the company in mind as I complete my tasks?
- Consider the impact of my attitude and decisions on co-workers?

Take the time to do this properly, writing down your answers. List some of the examples from your work performance that illustrate these qualities and add them to your job journal.

 These suggested questions are enough to get you started. Only *you* know the specifics of your job and the things that are important to your performance. Make sure you list examples relevant to your position.

 "Do not fear mistakes. There are none."

—Miles Davis

You are now starting to see your value as an individual in the organization. Remember as well that you are part of a team. You should consider your performance as a participating member of that team when evaluating your worth in an organization. Because employers are committed to streamlining their organizations, it is important that employees are team players, not only capable of working in a cooperative environment but excelling at it.

Ask yourself about your own abilities as a team player.

Am I:

- Cooperative?

- An effective listener?

- Supportive?

- Empathetic?

- A good communicator?

- Energetic?

- Flexible?

- Results oriented?

- A positive team player?

Organize staff events. For example, once a month someone could bring in a specialty tea or coffee for the office to enjoy.

Do I:

- Offer suggestions and positive feedback to co-workers when asked?
- Accept suggestions and feedback from co-workers?
- Respect the ideas and opinions of co-workers?
- Willingly accept my share of responsibility when things go wrong?
- Give credit where and when credit is due?
- Manage conflict in a mature and timely manner?
- Refuse to become involved in office gossip?

Again, take the time to jot down some concrete examples of these things and any others you can think of that relate to your work performance. By the time you are done with self-evaluation, you should have many more entries in your job journal.

Moving Forward

Even with all you do, can you still increase your worth and show you are a valuable asset to your company, one who deserves more money?
Yes.

 "The difference between a successful person and others is not a lack of strength, not a lack of knowledge, but rather a lack of will."

—Vincent T. Lombarch

How?

Train and retrain

When new systems that could improve your work become available, learn them. If there are workshops that will improve your effectiveness on the job, take them. You can never learn too much or know too much. Remember, companies consider your salary an exchange for knowledge. So the more knowledge you have, the more salary you are worth.

Be sure to document all courses, seminars, and in-service workshops you attend. Over the years it's easy to forget some of the things we have attended.

Crosstrain to become a generalist, not just a specialist

It is certainly wise to become an expert in your field and be very good at what you do. Unfortunately, if you are *too* narrowly focused on one job function you limit your possibilities for expansion. Employees who can offer expertise or skills in several areas are more valuable than those who are skilled in just one area. Once you are comfortable with your job duties, don't be afraid to expand your horizons and learn what goes on in the rest of the organization.

Be an idea generator

Look for ways to improve on the old ways of doing business instead of getting stuck in the trap of doing things one way simply because that is the way it has always been done. Don't be afraid of growth and change. Embrace innovation and see it for the exciting challenge it can be.

Never ask for solutions to problems without providing suggestions

Don't become known as the constant bearer of bad news. When there are problems to be overcome, spend time thinking about solutions rather than dwelling on the severity of the problem. A positive and proactive approach will be greatly appreciated and noticed by those you work for.

"We are continually faced by great opportunities brilliantly disguised as insolvable problems."

—Unknown

Be aware of the big picture

Sometimes, whether we mean to or not, we become caught up in the details of our job. In those instances we forget what it is we hope and need to accomplish. Take the time to re-focus periodically and remember where you and the organization are headed.

Do *not* get involved in office politics and company gossip

Unfortunately office gossip is a fact of life in the workplace. Don't get sucked into it, as no good can ever come of it. Steer clear of rumors, gossip, bickering, and backstabbing. Maintain a professional and positive attitude at all times. You never need to lower yourself to the standards of those who believe that the only way to get ahead is by holding others back.

Take on additional responsibilities

If you already have your workdays packed to the limit, obviously this isn't possible. If you aren't overworked and there are ways you can increase your responsibility level, do so. It will make you more valuable in the eyes of the company.

Remember, this means working efficiently, not just taking on tasks that eat up more of your time. Please see the chapter on *Work Hard, Play Hard.*

Work to learn, grow, and evolve in your job

Not only is your performance and attitude more positive and productive if you feel you are gaining from your position. It also lets your employers see you are gaining something from them as well. The employer-employee relationship is like any other relationship. It must be an **equal exchange**, where both parties reap the benefits.

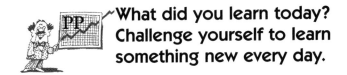
What did you learn today? Challenge yourself to learn something new every day.

Learn about government assistance

Find out about any available government grants or special funding that could help your company save money or provide training you may not otherwise have access to.

Set concrete and achievable goals with your employer

Many companies are now implementing a system called "pay at risk" or "variable pay." This means a portion of your salary is dependent on whether or not you meet the objectives you have established with your employer. You establish objectives to be met by a set date, and if you meet or exceed them, it is reflected in your salary.

These are not salary bonuses. A bonus is not necessarily performance-related and may be given at a variety of times such as Christmas, company year end, or when the company has made a particularly large profit.

Become proficient in a service your company contracts out

If your company spends money having someone outside the organization do desktop publishing work, work to improve your own desktop skills. It will save the company money and increase your value and worth to the organization.

"We learn to do something by doing it. There is no other way."

—John Holt

Fund-raise

If you work in not-for-profit industry, is it possible to plan fund-raising events to provide for a portion of your organization's or department's budget? This could potentially free up extra budget dollars for salary increases.

Save the company money

Nothing will endear you more to an organization than saving money. Always be on the look-out to save money, increase efficiency, or eliminate waste or redundancy. You may be surprised at how cost-effective even the smallest changes can be.

As you can see, getting a raise takes much more effort than simply waltzing into your employer's office and telling him or her how much of a salary increase you would like! In today's competitive job market, you must consistently work hard at improving your value in an organization—or the organization will leave you behind.

"In the middle of difficulty lies opportunity."

—Albert Einstein

Granted, every position is different. However, now that you know you need to start looking for ways to improve your performance, the performance of your department, and the overall performance of the company you work for, you're well on your way to improving your worth at work.

Self-evaluation is a tough job, but it is an essential part of determining if your price tag matches your job performance.

Every company has its own scale of rating what is valuable in an employee. Try and determine what your company or department considers essential qualities. Be sure to add *these* to your list of personal evaluation questions.

Go back and take a look at your job description. This may help you refocus as you evaluate your job performance. The description will give you more ideas of exactly what your employer is looking for in your position.

Determining why you feel you need or deserve a raise is another important step in this process. If you simply want more money because you would like to buy a new boat, take a longer tropical vacation this year, or start a college fund for your new baby, you will have a difficult time justifying a raise. These may be real concerns for *you*, but if you go into a meeting to ask for a raise armed with only the brochure for the new boat—and no concrete reasons for how you have earned this potential raise—you will probably be disappointed.

Did you complete all the tasks you set out to accomplish today? If not, do you know why you didn't meet your goal?

What Are You Worth?

Now that you have evaluated your motives, your performance, and your contributions at work, can you honestly say you are a valuable employee? Are you earning what you're worth and worth what you're earning? Or should your price tag be higher?

Comparative Shopping

Sitting down with a pencil and paper to evaluate your performance at work and determine whether or not you deserve more money is not only a difficult thing, it is also a very subjective thing. You have only your opinion to rely on, so you must try to be as honest and objective as possible.

Once you have worked through this process, you will certainly be more aware of your strengths and weaknesses. You will also know what aspects of your work personality you need to work on, develop, and improve. Will you know whether or not you should be paid more money for your strengths and contributions? You should probably have a better idea. And if you need more proof or reassurance that you deserve a raise, there are a few concrete things you can do.

"Life shrinks or expands in proportion to one's courage."

—Anais Nin

What?

1. Salary surveys
    Take it upon yourself to survey employees from different companies whose work is similar to yours. Is your salary comparable to theirs?

2. Industry standards
    Standard salary information is available for some industries in Labour Market Information Centres, government publications, or your local library. These resources can give you a general idea of salary ranges.

3. Benchmarking
    Benchmarking is a business term used to describe the process of continuously comparing and measuring an organization or an individual against others. This information is used to assist that organization or individual take action to improve overall performance.

4. Union regulations
    If you belong to a union, your salary will be fairly regulated. There should be little question of how much money you should be earning.

Keep track of all your efforts to gather information. This is excellent information to have with you when it comes time to negotiate a raise. It proves that you are not only interested, you are prepared.

What do these things mean to you as an employee? First of all, it means that you must be aware that more and more we are all employed in a global market. People are moving around the world to find employment, so your performance may be compared to people doing similar work half a world away. It is up to you to remain abreast of current trends and developments in your industry. Again, gaining additional knowledge makes you a more valuable and competitive employee.

Every so often, pick up a newspaper
from another city—or better yet,
another country—and glance
through it.

Take the time to learn how and where to benchmark. Look around at other individuals and organizations. What are they doing better than you and your organization? Are you prepared to change?

This may sound intimidating and overwhelming, but you will be surprised at the information and resources available to those interested enough to take the time to look.

What?

- Many industries have their own magazines or regular publications offering valuable information.

- Individual companies often provide bulletins or regular publications that highlight company changes, valuable employee contributions, and innovations in the industry.

- Many professions have groups that meet formally or informally to network and discuss industry advancements.

- Listen to the "buzz" at the office. What do other people know? Where do they get their information?

- Do you have access to the computer Internet? You may be amazed at the information available to those who know how to "surf the net."

- Remaining up-to-date on current affairs can often give you insight into where trends are headed and what consumers are demanding. You'll be tuned in to what's hot and what's not!

Did you learn something this week about the direction your job/company/industry will be taking in the future?

Granted, not everyone is interested in being the best in their industry or the frontrunner at work. Your own sense of ambition will obviously determine how much time and energy you spend staying on top of the changes in your profession.

Regardless of your competitive desires, however, you must remain valuable to your organization, not only so that you progressively earn more money, but simply to keep your job.

 Make an effort to join networking groups with others who are involved in your industry. This will help you remain "plugged in," and informed in your position.

It isn't necessary to lose sleep at night surfing the Internet for ideas on saving your department money, or perusing global newspapers for cost-cutting and time-saving measures. You should, however, remain current and aware of changes in your industry. Otherwise the industry will change and leave *you* behind.

Consistent benchmarking, even if done only casually, and regular salary surveys are ways of ensuring you remain competitively aware in a challenging job market.

Chapter 5

Asking For A Raise

You need to have courage, skill, and valid reasons for requesting more money. What's more, only a prepared and skilled person can convince an employer that he or she deserves more money.

Procrastination Terminators

Most people have a difficult time asking for a raise. They can therefore come up with a variety of reasons for why they shouldn't even approach their employer. Some interesting excuses are outlined here, as well as reasons why they should not be used.

Excuse	Excuse annihilator
1. No one else in my office has ever asked for a raise, so why should I?	If all your co-workers walked past a $100 bill, would you? Other people's lack of initiative and courage should not be the standard you follow. Become the example—be the first to ask.
2. Bob asked for a raise and he got turned down.	Bob's idea of a lunch break is an hour and a half, with an additional 20 minutes to digest! Maybe he didn't deserve one!
3. I don't think the company has enough money.	When did you become the company accountant?

4. I've only been with the company for two years. I'll wait one more.

Maybe you should wait another 18 and get your retirement bonus and gold watch all at the same time!

5. My boss is too busy. I'll wait until things slow down.

Have you ever worked for a boss who isn't busy? It's your boss's job to deal with all aspects of business, and employees requesting raises is one of them.

6. I'm too scared. What if they say no?

If you spend your life not trying things because they may not go your way, you won't do much. Your boss had the chance to say "no" to hiring you, but said "yes." Maybe she will again now.

7. I don't know what to say.

Continue reading and you will be prepared to request a raise confidently.

"Procrastination is the thief of time."

—Edward Young

Forget creating excuses. Your time and effort is better spent increasing your worth at work. The end result may be more profitable than you hoped. You just have to ask. The worst thing that can happen is your employer says "no." You'll never know until you try!

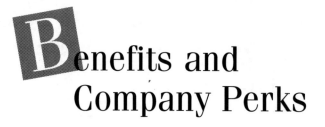

Benefits and Company Perks

Before you ask for an increase in your wage, consider requesting additional benefits or perks. The benefits you receive from your company are often tax exempt, and more benefits may mean more of your salary can be used for other things.

"Difficulties strengthen the mind,
as labor does the body."

—Lucius Seneca

Consider requesting:

- Extra holidays. These could be extra paid holidays or the approval to take a leave without pay.
- Travel expenses. These could include a car allowance, mileage reimbursements, meals, entertainment, and/or accommodations.
- Expense account
- Company pension plan
- Healthcare insurance
- Company vehicle
- Life insurance
- Company shares or stocks
- Disability insurance
- Profit-sharing
- Dental insurance
- Pay bonuses
- Hospitalization coverage
- Group savings plans
- Parking
- Incentive packages
- Moving expenses

Although these sorts of benefits may not show up on your next paycheck, in the long run they will translate into more money in your pocket.

Salary Expectations

If you want a salary increase, then you need to know exactly how much money you will ask for. "The most you can give" may be what you would like to say, but it is probably not the best way to approach things.

"A little tact and wise management may often evade resistance, and carry a point, where direct force might be in vain."

—Anonymous

Every company has their own method for calculating employee pay increases. Some companies base increases on inflation rates, while others consider what competitors are doing. Most companies take the overall economy into account. *All* companies bear in mind how they are doing financially. As you can see, there is a lot to consider.

Many companies have a maximum allowable pay increase. Contact your human resources department to see if your company has one and how much it is.

Unless you are an accountant or an economist and sit on the company board of directors, it will be difficult to know *exactly* how much you should request. Although the amount will depend on your circumstances, you can make an informed and intelligent guess.

Circumstance 1: No change in job description; no cost-of-living increase.

If your job description has remained the same and you have not received a cost-of-living increase, you can use inflation and cost-of-living rates as your guide.

When using cost-of-living and inflation rates as the foundation for your calculations, explain to your employer that you are simply keeping your salary on par with the economy and not jumping ahead.

Using these set rates, calculating how much to ask for is straightforward.

Example

Chris is currently earning $26,500 per year and is requesting a wage increase. The current increase in the cost of living rate is 4.2 percent, and the inflation rate is 6 percent.

These rates are calculated four times per year and may be obtained through your local employment center.

Calculation:

Salary × (Cost of living + Inflation) = Desired Increase
$26,500 × (4.2% + 6%) =
$26,500 × 10.2% =
$2703 = Desired Increase

Remember: approaching your employer with a slightly higher figure will give you some room to negotiate.

$2703 × 5% = Reasonable request
$2838 = Reasonable request

This is a **reasonable** figure to have in mind when you approach your employer, but be prepared to negotiate. Your employer will want to keep your increase to a minimum, while still keeping you happy.

Circumstance 2: *No change in job description; received a cost-of-living increase.*

This calculation will not be as straightforward. You are now requesting a **performance-related raise**. How much you request will depend on how much you *deserve* it.

You honestly evaluated whether or not you deserve a raise in chapter 4. Now you must judge how much of a raise you think is reasonable. Remember, you can do your own salary survey inside and outside your organization to give you a better idea of the industry standard for your position.

When customers or clients compliment you, write down what they say in your job journal.

Whether you decide to request a 1 percent or a 10 percent increase, you must convince your *employer* your performance warrants this increase.

Circumstance 3: *Your job description has changed.*

If your job description has changed, this is an excellent time to request a raise. Clearly your employer feels you are ready to take on more responsibility. Many employers will automatically give you a pay increase as well, but if they don't, it is up to you to ask for one.

When given a change in duties, request a raise immediately. If you have not yet asked, then request an increase as soon as possible.

Before you request a specific amount, do some research.

✔ Find out what other people who are doing similar jobs are paid. Contact:

- Your human resources department

- Competitors' human resources departments

- Employment centers

Ask for the salary range for the type of work you are now doing. Remember: not everyone who does the same job will be paid the same, but the range should be similar.

✔ Consider how long you have been doing your new job and how your work compares to others. Make an educated guess as to where you think you should fall in the salary range.

Example

You have now been doing your new job for two months, but had assumed some of the new responsibilities prior to being formally assigned the position. You know more than someone who is totally green.

You should request a salary toward the lower end of the range, but not the least amount. Although your experience warrants a slightly higher request, you are not yet an expert. If the salary range for the position is $33,000 to $42,000, approach your employer with a wage of $34,000 to $35,000 in mind.

Your salary request should *not* be based on what you received before. Your request should reflect your new job description and the pay normally associated with it.

Trying to determine how much to ask for can be difficult. If you ask for *too much*, you may offend your employer. If on the other hand you ask for *too little*, you are selling yourself short. Try to be objective and reasonable when deciding how much to ask for.

"Trades would not take place unless it were advantageous to the parties concerned. Of course, it is better to strike as good a bargain as one's bargaining position admits. The worst outcome is when by overriding greed, no bargain is struck, and a trade that could have been advantageous to both parties, does not come off at all."

—Benjamin Franklin

Planning Your Raise Request

Everything you do at work and your value to the company may be clear to you, but they may not be clear to your employer. You must convince your employer that you *deserve* the raise you are asking for. This takes time, effort, and planning.

"The man who does not work for the love of work but only for money is not likely to make money nor to find much fun in life."

—Charles M. Schwab

The Why Of It All

Prepare yourself to tell your employer *why* you deserve a raise. You will be much more effective if you describe why you are a valuable employee who deserves a wage increase, rather than describing why your sporting equipment needs to be replaced.

Refer to the chapter *Who Gets the Raise* if you have trouble coming up with reasons.

Think of as many convincing reasons as possible. Your time is better spent planning for several weeks and providing convincing arguments than rushing in, being turned down, and having to wait several months before you can ask again.

Write out your reasons for requesting a raise, and take your list to your meeting with your employer.

Example

- I am a more experienced electrician than a year ago.

- I bring in new business.

- I have a positive attitude that makes customers return.

- I take initiative and am a hard worker.

 Write down all the reasons you can think of. Don't stop at five or six because you think that's good enough. It may be the tenth reason you think of that convinces your employer.

Supporting Arguments

Providing concrete examples to support your reasons is crucial. Saying "I am a better employee because . . ." is much more convincing than just saying you are better—and leaving your employer to guess why.

 It is essential that you are prepared to tell an employer how you do your job and why you do it well. You need to convince employers of your worth.

Be prepared *before* you go into your boss's office, so you can back statements you make with specifics.

How?

Provide concrete examples

Expand on your reasons for wanting a raise, and describe why and how they are true. If you say you take initiative, describe the things you do that go above and beyond your job requirements. If you say you bring in new clients, elaborate by saying how you got them or how much business they have done with the company. These are the supporting statements that will convince employers that what you say is true.

 Base your reasons for requesting a raise on facts, not on emotions. "I deserve a raise because . . ." is much more convincing than "I need one because . . ."

Develop a job journal

Keep track of your accomplishments. Write down the specific things you have done and the contributions you have made to your company, complete with details and dates.

Example

Sept 9: RJ Simmons from Blacks Computers said I was one of the few people he could count on to provide fast and accurate repairs for customers. RJ calls me first when customers are looking for help.

Oct 5: Attended a workshop called "What's new in the world of computers." I learned about new installation techniques and discovered QQ Computers is competing with us for customers.

 Once you discover what a valuable tool a job journal is, you will wonder how you ever got a raise without it.

Use your job journal to keep track of:

✔ Projects you have worked on and done well

✔ Ideas for improving the company

✔ Compliments you receive from clients, co-workers, and supervisors

✔ Letters of recommendation you receive

✔ Things you have done to boost office morale

✔ Things you do to promote the company

✔ Courses and workshops you attend, complete with certificates

✔ Money-saving and money-making ideas

✔ Any other information which reflects the good work you are doing

 Before you approach your employer, summarize or highlight your job journal so you don't have to flip through it when you want to give examples. Categorize the things you have done, such as compliments, ideas, or money-saving strategies, so you can easily refer to them during your discussion.

This information will be invaluable when it comes time to develop your rationale for a raise. You can flip through your journal and be reminded of what you have done since your last pay increase . . . Then you can remind your employer.

Focus on your value as an employee

No doubt many people have skills and credentials similar to yours and could be trained to do your job. However, it would be difficult and costly for an employer to find someone who is already trained in their procedures, knowledgeable about their company, and committed to helping them prosper. You are a valuable asset to your organization.

Continuing to train, learn, and grow makes you even more valuable. Now is your opportunity to prove to your employer that you can continue to develop your skills and work hard to serve the company the best way possible.

Describe the steps you take to stay on top of things and be a productive employee. Use your **Process Planner** to help describe what you do to stay current.

Remember, a Process Planner is your record of things you regularly do to improve your performance and worth to the company.

Your Process Planner should outline:

✔ The things you do to improve your work environment

✔ How you followed through on ideas

✔ Your strategies for improving your work

✔ Things you did to make your workday or week go smoother

✔ Things you want to accomplish and how you go about doing them

✔ Goals you set for yourself

 Describe why you are a better employee as a result of the things you have done. Outline the goals you are currently working toward to show that you are continuing to work hard and grow.

By describing the plans you make and follow through on, employers can see how much effort and enthusiasm you put into your job. This demonstrates your continuing effort to develop your talents and your commitment to growing as an employee.

 Review your Process Planner before you meet with your employer. It will remind you how much you are doing.

Your Accomplishment Summary

Summarize the things you have done into a concrete list you can refer to when speaking with your employer.

Use the work space below to summarize your work.

Objectives You Set For Yourself

_____

_____

_____

_____

_____

How You Accomplished Them

_____

_____

_____

_____

_____

Goals Currently Working On

_____

_____

_____

_____

_____

Accomplishments

_____

_____

_____

_____

_____

*Recognition From Co-workers, Supervisors,
and Clients*

_____
_____
_____
_____
_____

How You Contributed to The Company

_____
_____
_____
_____
_____

How You Affected Office Morale

_____
_____
_____
_____
_____

Ways You Saved the Company Money

_____
_____
_____
_____
_____

Ways You Made the Company Money

_____
_____
_____
_____
_____

_____

_____

_____

_____

_____

reparing For The Big Day

Now that you are organized and have a summary of your accomplishments and contributions, you are *almost* ready for your meeting. There are only a few final details to consider before you approach your employer.

Who To Ask

Asking the right person is essential to getting the right answer. Don't waste your time convincing a co-worker that you deserve a raise when they don't have the power to give you one. If you feel you need the practice discussing all the reasons you deserve more money, that's fine. Just don't do so much practicing that you never get around to really asking.

 "Trust that still, small voice that says, 'This might work and I'll try it'."

—Diane Mariechild

Find out who is responsible for handling raise requests. While the accounting department issues your paycheck, they probably aren't the people to see when requesting more money.

It may seem logical to go straight to the top with something as important as a raise request, but bypassing the regular chain of command is frowned upon in most companies.

Begin with your immediate supervisor. Have everything prepared before your meeting and begin by stating you are formally requesting a pay increase. If they do not have the authority to grant you more money, they will refer you to the person who can help you.

 Even if you know your supervisor doesn't have the authority to grant raises, inform them of your intentions. They may be able to help your case by telling the manager what a great worker they think you are. And it will show them that you are considerate enough of their position to keep them in the "loop" of communication.

What's more, your supervisor may have inside knowledge that can improve your chances of being granted a raise. They may tell you to wait a week until the company receives word on a new project or recommend waiting because M. Brown had a bad week. Your supervisor can also reassure you that you *do* deserve more money for the great job you do and there is no time like the present to ask.

Whoever you approach, make sure you do it in a positive manner. You never know who your boss talks to before making their final decision.

Timing, Timing, Timing

Schedule an appointment so that both you and your employer have set aside time to discuss your request. Dropping by your boss's office just as she is leaving for a meeting does not present a very professional impression. If you don't consider a raise request important enough to bother scheduling a convenient meeting time, why should she?

 Scheduling a formal appointment demonstrates that you respect your employer's time. It also suggests that you are prepared and want uninterrupted time for discussion.

Give yourself ample time to convince your employer of your worth. Having to stop halfway through your discussion because you have a class to teach does not reflect well on your planning abilities.

Unfortunately, your timing has more impact on whether or not you receive a raise than it should. Employers are human and companies experience ups and downs. You need to remember this when planning your meeting.

Consider

1. Have you recently completed a difficult project or received a positive performance review?

    If so, this would be an excellent time to request a raise. Your superb performance is fresh in your employer's mind. It will take much less effort to convince your boss you deserve more money.

2. Is your company currently making or losing money?

    Your request is more likely to be granted when the company is making money, but you can still try even when a company is losing money.

Why?

• Some companies "lose" money to keep their taxes to a minimum.

Example

When a corporation has one company which is making money, it may see to it that another loses money. This lowers the taxes the corporation must pay. Believe it or not, if this is happening, it may actually be a good time to request a raise.

- The company may be acquiring new equipment or buying out other companies. Their financial statement shows a negative profit, although they are really expanding. Again, this is a good time to request a raise.

Outline those activities you have performed that your supervisor seemed especially pleased with.

- If you request a raise and are turned down, you may be first in line once things turn around. It is hard for a company to continue saying "no" to a valuable employee.

3. Is the budget for next year still being developed?

    It is a good idea to approach your employer before the budget is finalized. Extra money may be allocated to salaries. If you wait, there may be no surplus in the salary budget to grant your request.

4. How long has it been since your last raise?

- If it has only been three weeks since you received your annual cost-of-living increase, you may want to consider waiting. Don't give your employer the chance to say, "You just got a raise, that's good enough for now."

Cost-of-living increases are not the same as performance-related requests. When cost-of-living raises are given, every employee receives them. Only employees who work hard and request performance raises receive them.

- If you received a **performance-related increase** only a few months ago, consider waiting. Only if you have done something exceptionally well, have saved the company a huge amount of money, or have been given a change in responsibilities should you ask for more money so soon.

- If you previously requested a raise and it was declined, consider the reasons before deciding when to ask again.

  - If your company was in a financial bind, wait until things improve. Once things are on the upswing, ask again. This could mean waiting six weeks or six months.

  - Your employer asked you to improve certain areas of your performance before your request was granted. If your performance has improved, ask again. Your performance, not the calendar, should be your guide.

 Make a conscious effort to incorporate customer, co-worker, and supervisory feedback into your everyday work.

  - The company asked you to wait three months. When those three months have passed, go back and ask again.

No matter how long it has been since your last raise, if you feel you have done enough to warrant more money, ask. Time is not the deciding factor. What you have done in that time is.

5. Is your company hiring or firing employees?

    If the current goal of employees in your company is simply keeping their jobs, you may want to wait. If the company is hiring more staff, however, now is your opportunity to act. Be sensitive to the issues and concerns of your company.

6. How is your state of mind?

    If you are having a difficult time at work or are experiencing a crisis in your personal life, wait to approach your employer. Difficult times may be reflected in your enthusiasm, as well as in your self-confidence. You want to appear positive and productive when requesting a raise.

You want to prove to your employer you *deserve* a raise, not that you *need* one. Raises usually reflect productivity, not personal necessity.

7. How is your employer's state of mind?

    If things are unusually busy at work, your boss is frantically completing a project with deadlines, or she is headed off on holidays soon, wait a few days or weeks before requesting your raise. Your efforts will be better spent when your employer has the time and interest to consider what you say.

Choosing an appropriate time for your meeting can be critical to securing a salary increase. Be conscious of the time you choose.

Assemble Relevant Documents

Gather together all the appropriate information you will need to prove your case. If at all possible, be prepared to show your employer those documents that illustrate just how valuable you are.

What?

✔ **Performance Reviews.** Favorable reviews show that your employer already believes you are a valuable employee. Remind him or her how your performance has been rated in the past.

 Favorable performance reviews are only one method of proving your worth. Be careful to not say "You said . . . so you have to give me a raise." Your next review may not be quite so good if you do this.

✔ **Job Journal**. Although you might already have written summaries, take your job journal in case your employer wants to look through it.

✔ **Process Planner**. Be prepared to show your employer your process planner.

Your employer may be so impressed with your job journal and process planner that she recommends other employees use similar tools. If that happens, it's one more productive idea to add to your journal.

✔ **Sales Charts.** Show how you have affected sales since your last raise. Chart for your employer how much money the company makes as a result of your excellent performance.

✔ **Letters of Recommendation.** These can be formal or informal letters from people who are satisfied with your work.

Save the thank-you cards and letters of appreciation you receive. Not only are they useful when it comes time to request a raise, they can be used to boost your morale on a bad day.

✔ **Descriptions of How You Saved the Company Money.** Companies are in business to make money. Show how your efforts are helping to increase their profits.

✔ Anything else that shows how your efforts and your attitude affect the company in a positive way.

By gathering together and presenting the relevant documents, you show your employer that you take your request seriously, that you believe strongly in your performance and value, and that you have taken the time to convince your employer of your merit. Your preparation shows that you take all aspects of your work seriously.

Lookin' Good,
Feelin' Good

Although you see your employer on a regular basis, it is a good idea to look your best when requesting more money. How you look influences how people react to you, and you want it to have a positive influence on the day of your appointment.

Dress Appropriately

If you have an outfit that is especially appropriate and makes you feel particularly confident, wear it. You want to give the best impression possible on the day of your raise request.

Be sure that whatever you choose to wear to your appointment is comfortable. There is nothing worse than being a little nervous and having that feeling compounded because you feel like your skirt is gaping when you sit or that your shirt is too tight around your stomach.

Try your outfit on the night before your meeting. Walk, sit, and stand in it. Is it clean and comfortable? Does it convey the image you want it to project?

 "Adventures don't begin until you get into the forest. That first step is an act of faith."

—Mickey Hart

Personal Grooming

Whether you work in construction or in a law firm, be sure to be clean and neat when you show up for your raise request meeting. This entails a shower, shave, deodorant, and only the most sparing use of cologne or perfume.

This may sound silly, but you want to be sure your skills and contribution to the organization have an impact—not your aroma!

Look Rested

The night before your meeting, don't stay up to watch the late movie on television. It is unprofessional to yawn during any meeting, but particularly the one where you are telling your employer how much effort you put in on the job.

 You want the makeup you wear to highlight your features, not hide the bags under your eyes.

Body Language

Make a conscious effort to sit up straight and look your employer in the eye when you are speaking. This will make you appear confident and assured, whether you are nervous on the inside or not. Smile and maintain your sense of humor. It will help relax you and set a good tone for your meeting.

Pay attention to any nervous gestures or habits you might have. We are often unaware of these, and you may need a friend or co-worker to tell you if you have any distracting habits. It is very disconcerting to be in a meeting with people who constantly click their pen, bite their nails, twist their hair, or endlessly roll their tie up and down. You want your employer to be focused on what you are *saying*, not your nervous habits.

 Remember these habits also have a nasty way of creeping into our speech when we are nervous. Be very aware of using "umm," "like," "you know," or any other repetitive phrases. These serve only to distract from what you are saying.

Feel Good

Review your performance reviews and read your job journal and process planner summaries. Remind yourself of what a good employee you are and the valuable things you do. This will make you feel more confident when you approach your employer.

Before your meeting, practice describing how your work benefits the company. The more times you say it, the easier it will be to say it to your employer with confidence.

If you go into the meeting with a positive attitude, focusing only on a positive outcome, it will "reflect" in your presentation and your overall confidence level. This positive outlook is contagious and will affect your employer's impression of you.

Treat your request for a raise as you would a formal job interview. Plan, prepare, and give it your best shot. The results will be worth it.

he Opening Line

You are ready for your meeting! You are well-dressed, well-rested, and prepared with all relevant information and examples. And you are ready for a positive outcome.

What on Earth Do You Say to Get the Meeting Underway?

No matter how much you feel you deserve more money for the work you do, you can still have a very difficult time bringing up the topic of money.

Here are some suggestions for how you can ease your way into what will surely be a great meeting.

1. I feel my experience level has increased significantly over the past eight months of work, making me a considerably more valuable employee. As a result, I would like to negotiate an increase in my salary at this time.

2. Over the past year, my effectiveness in the organization has improved in a number of ways. I would like to negotiate a salary increase that would accurately reflect that improvement.

3. I have asked you to meet with me today to discuss some of the concrete ways I have contributed to the organization. With these effi-

ciencies I have identified in mind, I would like to negotiate an increase in my salary.

4. Given that my responsibility level at work has recently increased, I would like to discuss a coinciding increase in my salary.

5. I've scheduled this meeting with you today to renegotiate my salary.

Keep in mind that these are simply suggestions and your situation is unique. Whatever opening line you decide on, remember that you have worked hard to be where you are. You have planned, prepared, and progressed, and you have nothing to lose by asking!

How Bad Could It Be?

So the boss said "no" to your raise request, and you're left wondering why. Well, there's an excellent place to begin. If you have put in the time and effort, gathered up your courage, and taken the plunge to ask for more money, you should not consider the event complete until you know the reasons for the outcome—whether they are positive or negative.

"It is not because things are difficult that we do not dare; it is because we do not dare that they are difficult."

—Seneca

Asking for a raise can be a stressful experience. Presumably you wouldn't ask for one simply for the fun of doing it. You *honestly* feel your performance at work is worth a salary increase.

If your boss has said "no" to your request, it would appear there is a bit of a communication gap or a difference of opinion about your work habits. Or maybe things are financially tight within the company. There is no point asking for more money in the future if you don't understand and correct or improve upon the reasons you didn't receive an increase this time.

Have you made any or all of the suggested improvements in your performance since your last meeting regarding salary expectations?

After the No

There are a number of ways to handle yourself if your request for a raise has been turned down

You . . . run from the office fighting back angry tears.
Your boss . . . happily resumes work, glad to have not had to explain anything to you.

You . . . become furiously angry and loudly demand more money—or else!
Your boss . . . calls security and has you physically removed from the building.

You . . . begin to whine about how much your mortgage is, how big your alimony payments are, and that you just can't afford the golf club membership you really wanted.
Your boss . . . makes a mental note to have more Kleenex available in her office.

You . . . rave that Alex in the widget department just got a salary increase after only nine months of being with the company.
Your boss . . . suggests that perhaps you could golf as Alex's guest when he gets his club membership.

You . . . become defensive and point out with a sneer that your supervisor's son probably makes more money working part-time in the office than you do.
Your boss . . . makes a note to never buy Girl Scout cookies from your daughter again.

Make note of those situations where you have managed confrontation or constructive criticism in a positive and professional manner. Incorporate what you learned into your regular work habits.

You . . . lecture your boss on the merit of your work and your loyalty to the company, pointing out that if you don't get a raise you'll quit.

Your boss . . . suggests you notify the mailroom so they can save some boxes for you when you clean out your office.

You . . . tell your boss that you appreciate her candid honesty and ask if she would please explain the reasons behind her decision.

Your boss . . . asks if you would like a coffee before you begin your discussion.

Whatever your reaction, it is *your* responsibility to get the whole story so you can make appropriate changes that will warrant a salary increase the next time you ask. As always, it is pointless to go through an experience if you fail to learn from it.

"Take your life in your own hands and what happens? A terrible thing: no one to blame."

—Erica Jong

So now what?

Feedback, Feedback, Feedback

Do not be discouraged and angry if you do not get a raise. Instead, consider this a starting point. You have requested feedback about your performance at work in the form of money and it has been turned down. As a result, you now know you probably need to make some changes.

It is always possible that the company simply doesn't have the budget to offer you a salary increase. Even if this is the case, take the opportunity to ask for feedback on your work efforts.

Ideally you should be prepared before your meeting for the possibility your request may be denied.

HOW?

1. Consider the possibility that your employer may turn down your request. How will you feel if the answer is "no"?

 If you are granted a pay increase, maintain a professional attitude with co-workers. Comparing your salary increase to others' or telling a co-worker whose request was denied can create tension in the workplace.

2. Come prepared with questions to help you and your employer honestly evaluate your performance and the basis of their decision.

WHAT?

- Why was my request denied?
- How can I improve my performance so I'll get a raise next time?
- What criteria are used to determine who receives a raise?
- When would it be appropriate to ask again?

3. If you sense that you will not be able to ask your questions immediately after your request is denied, schedule a meeting *within the next week* to further discuss the reasons you were turned down.

4. Prepare a list of ideas and suggestions for how your work performance could be improved.

5. Make a point of scheduling a follow-up meeting to reevaluate your progress. It could be six weeks or six months, depending on what you need to work on. This need not be a salary-related meeting.

Regularly jot down in your job journal the positive efforts you are making to improve your performance. It is much easier to make note of them when they happen, as opposed to trying to think of them on demand.

You have already gone through the process of evaluating yourself objectively prior to asking for a raise. Now you need to do it again with the assistance of your employer. It is important that you have a well thought out opinion of your work performance, but when it comes to salary, it is ultimately your employer's opinion that matters most. All the questions you have asked yourself about your own performance at work will now be discussed with your employer.

"Did you ever observe to whom the accidents happen? Chance favors only the prepared mind."

—Louis Pasteur

Be open-minded and objective when listening to your employer's thoughts and opinions. Most importantly, give yourself some time to reflect on what has been discussed before reacting to it. You will be asking for both positive and negative feedback. Be sure you are prepared to hear both.

Keep in mind that getting a raise can be a slow process. You may have to go through a process of learning and growing in order to qualify for an increase in pay. Remember, your relationship with your employer is one of exchange—skills and knowledge for money. As your knowledge and skill level increases, so should your salary.

Say What?

For your easy reference, here are some of the terms and buzzwords that appear in this book, some of which may be new to you. Business frequently has its own language, and it is important for you to stay current.

Dishabituation: The process in which we begin once again to react to an experience we have become used to.

Habituation: The process in which people are exposed to an experience so often that they become bored and no longer notice or react to it.

Pay at Risk/ Variable Pay: A portion of your salary that is dependent on your achieving the goals and objectives you have set with your employer. This type of pay scheme is often reserved for management or executives.

Benchmarking: The process of observing and comparing yourself and your company to others in the industry in order to determine where you stand in the field. This is done not to frustrate you but to give you ideas on where to improve yourself and your company, to make you more competitive.

Salary Bonus: A money bonus given to you that is not necessarily performance-based.

Generalist: An employee with a working knowledge of a broad range of duties within a company or department.

"I learn by going where I have to go."

—Theodore Roethke

Specialist: An employee with very specific knowledge related to only one position or aspect of that position.

That Was Then ...

- You received your annual raise like clockwork.

- You received a regular bonus at Christmas or at the end of the year.

- Benefits were something you expected, in addition to your salary raises.

- It was rare that part of your salary was totally dependent on whether or not you met the objectives the company set for you.

- You weren't expected to ask for a raise. If you deserved one, the company would approach you and offer it.

- Anything new you needed to learn was taught to you by the company.

- Salary meant only the money you took home in dollars.

- Your salary was almost guaranteed to rise with the cost of living.

This Is Now ...

- Employers consider all company perks such as company car, health benefits, fitness membership options to be part of your salary.

- Employers *do* offer training, but you are expected to take the time to keep current with changes and advancements in your industry.

- Employers do not guarantee that your salary will increase yearly, even if the cost of living is on the rise.

- If you have worked hard, met your objectives, and grown within the company you are still expected to take the initiative to ask for a raise.

- Up to 50 percent of your salary may be dependent on your reaching objectives you have set with your employer.

- The amount of money you make is often directly related to the knowledge you have to offer the company.

- Employees are expected to pay a part of the cost of their benefit package.

- If you save the company money, it can directly affect the amount of money you take home.

"True life is lived when tiny changes occur."

—Leo Tolstoy

Conclusion

You are on your way to not only becoming a better *paid* employee, but also a *better* employee. Who would have thought that the process of requesting a raise could help you learn so much about yourself and help you develop your value as an employee?

Once you have secured your raise, you must continue to set goals, work hard, and prove that you deserve the extra money. The next time you request more money, your employer will know that you continue giving your best even after receiving a raise.

"What lies behind us and what lies before us are tiny matters, compared to what lies within us."

—Ralph Waldo Emerson

Congratulations. Your efforts and value as an employee are sure to be rewarded.

VGM CAREER BOOKS

CAREER DIRECTORIES
Careers Encyclopedia
Dictionary of Occupational Titles
Occupational Outlook Handbook

CAREERS FOR
Animal Lovers
Bookworms
Caring People
Computer Buffs
Crafty People
Culture Lovers
Environmental Types
Fashion Plates
Film Buffs
Foreign Language Aficionados
Good Samaritans
Gourmets
Health Nuts
History Buffs
Kids at Heart
Nature Lovers
Night Owls
Number Crunchers
Plant Lovers
Shutterbugs
Sports Nuts
Travel Buffs
Writers

CAREERS IN
Accounting; Advertising; Business;
Child Care; Communications;
Computers; Education;
Engineering;
the Environment; Finance;
Government; Health Care; High
Tech; International Business;
Journalism; Law; Marketing;
Medicine; Science; Social &
Rehabilitation Services

CAREER PLANNING
Beating Job Burnout
Beginning Entrepreneur
Career Planning & Development for
    College Students &
    Recent Graduates
Career Change
Careers Checklists
College and Career Success for
    Students with Learning Disabilities
Complete Guide to Career Etiquette
Cover Letters They Don't Forget
Dr. Job's Complete Career Guide
Executive Job Search Strategies

Guide to Basic Cover Letter
    Writing
Guide to Basic Résumé Writing
Guide to Internet Job Searching
Guide to Temporary Employment
Job Interviewing for College
    Students
Joyce Lain Kennedy's Career Book
Out of Uniform
Slam Dunk Résumés
The Parent's Crash Course in
    Career Planning: Helping Your
    College Student Succeed

CAREER PORTRAITS
Animals; Cars; Computers;
Electronics; Fashion;
Firefighting; Music; Nursing;
Sports; Teaching; Travel; Writing

GREAT JOBS FOR
Business Majors
Communications Majors
Engineering Majors
English Majors
Foreign Language Majors
History Majors
Psychology Majors

HOW TO
Apply to American Colleges and
    Universities
Approach an Advertising Agency and
    Walk Away with the Job You Want
Be a Super Sitter
Bounce Back Quickly After
    Losing Your Job
Change Your Career
Choose the Right Career
Cómo escribir un currículum vitae
    en inglés que tenga éxito
Find Your New Career Upon
    Retirement
Get & Keep Your First Job
Get Hired Today
Get into the Right Business School
Get into the Right Law School
Get into the Right Medical School
Get People to Do Things Your Way
Have a Winning Job Interview
Hit the Ground Running in Your
    New Job
Hold It All Together When You've
    Lost Your Job
Improve Your Study Skills
Jumpstart a Stalled Career

Land a Better Job
Launch Your Career in TV News
Make the Right Career Moves
Market Your College Degree
Move from College into a
    Secure Job
Negotiate the Raise You Deserve
Prepare Your Curriculum Vitae
Prepare for College
Run Your Own Home Business
Succeed in Advertising When all
    You Have Is Talent
Succeed in College
Succeed in High School
Take Charge of Your Child's Early
    Education
Write a Winning Résumé
Write Successful Cover Letters
Write Term Papers & Reports
Write Your College Application Essay

MADE EASY
Cover Letters
Getting a Raise
Job Hunting
Job Interviews
Résumés

OPPORTUNITIES IN
This extensive series provides
detailed information on nearly 150
individual career fields.

RÉSUMÉS FOR
Advertising Careers
Architecture and Related Careers
Banking and Financial Careers
Business Management Careers
College Students &
    Recent Graduates
Communications Careers
Education Careers
Engineering Careers
Environmental Careers
Ex-Military Personnel
50+ Job Hunters
Government Careers
Health and Medical Careers
High School Graduates
High Tech Careers
Law Careers
Midcareer Job Changes
Re-Entering the Job Market
Sales and Marketing Careers
Scientific and Technical Careers
Social Service Careers
The First-Time Job Hunter

VGM Career Horizons
a division of *NTC Publishing Group*
4255 West Touhy Avenue
Lincolnwood, Illinois 60646–1975